NEW

Super Pig and Jip the pirate

Illustrated by
Nina O'Connell

M
Macmillan Education

Super Pig

Look at me.
I am Super Pig.
I am going to Deb's party.
Fat Pig sat down to wait
for Sam and Meg.
He went to sleep. Zzzzzz.

Look at me.

What can I see.

I can see Sam.

I will help him.

I am Super Pig.

Look at me.
What can I see.
Jip is in the fire.
I will help him.
Here comes Super Pig.

Look at me.
What can I see.
I can see Ben.
I will help him.
I am Super Pig.

Look at me.
I can see Deb.
I can help Deb too.
I am Super Pig.

What can I see now.
There is Meg.
I will help her.
Here comes Super Pig.

Come on Fat Pig.
Get up.
It is time to go
to Deb's party.

Jip the pirate

Jip was going to Deb's party.

I will be a pirate, he said.

I will have a red coat.

I will have a big hat.

I will have big boots.

Jip sat down to wait for
Fat Pig and Ben and Meg.
He went to sleep.
Zzzzzz. Zzzzzz. Zzzzzz.

Jip was on a pirate ship.
The ship had a pirate flag.
The pirates had a map.
They wanted to find the gold.

Where is the gold, said Jip.
I don't know, said Meg.
You must ask Ben.

Where is the gold, said Jip.
I don't know, said Ben.
You must ask Fat Pig.

Where is the gold, said Jip.
I don't know, said Fat Pig.
Then you must walk the plank,
said Jip.

Fat Pig got on the plank.
Go on. Go on, said Jip.
Fat Pig was just going to
fall into the water . . . .

Bang. Bang. Bang.

Come on Jip, said Meg.

Get up.

It is time to go to the party.